SOLO JAZZ GUITAR

THE COMPLETE CHORD MELODY METHOD

T0039904

ISBN-13: 978-1-4234-2276-1
ISBN-10: 1-4234-2276-7

HAL•LEONARD® CORPORATION

7777 W. BLUEMOUND RD. P.O. BOX 13819 MILWAUKEE, WI 53213

Visit Hal Leonard Online at
www.halleonard.com

SPECIAL THANKS

My very special thanks to the following people: Mike Stern, Steve Khan, Scott Henderson, Jimmy Herring, Wayne Krantz, Adam Nitti, Nite Driscoll, Randy Hoexter, T.J. Pattillo, Jeff Spencer, Huston and Kelly Singletary, and Shane Theriot for their continued support as fellow musicians and friends; the students attending the Atlanta Institute of Music for teaching me as much as I teach them; my mother, Kathy Corby, and family—Tracy and Ricky Dyal, Ted and Maria Corby, Ginger and Wes Boatwright, Leann and Brent Lewis; my nieces and nephews—Clint, Tiffany, Brittany, Amanda, Ashleigh, April, Matt, Chris, BJ, and Billy for their love and support; my brother, sister-in-law, and niece, David, Rachel, and Lauren Bodne who continually go above and beyond to support me; my mother-in-law Maureen Rosenbaum for her uplifting spirit; to Brian Monaghan for just being you; to all the staff of the Atlanta Institute of Music who are great players and teachers—my forever friends Ron McDowell, Rick Stewart, John, Fiona, Miles, and Ella Grindy, Daryl Murray, Tim Meredith, and Mike and Karen Welford; to my brother and sister in faith, Adam and Stephanie Nitti; and a very special thanks to God for making all things possible.

ACKNOWLEDGMENTS

The Atlanta Institute of Music (Nite Driscoll, Angie Harrison, and Steve Freeman)

Liquid Blue (Adam Nitti, Tom Knight, Sam Skelton)

Brian Moore Custom Guitars (Patrick Cummings, Susi Cummings)

Mesa Boogie Amps (Shawn Beressord)

DEDICATION

To: My best friend, Jim Gilligan, who is no longer with us.

My father-in-law, Larry Rosenbaum, who was a fine musician, professor, and loving father.

My wife Kristin Hart and daughter Sara Jessica Hart

CONTENTS

ABOUT THE AUTHOR

Canadian born and raised, Bill Hart started out listening and playing blues. At 15 years of age, he moved to the U.S. (Jacksonville, Florida) where he played in jam sessions with many professional players including Alan Collins and the Van Zants. From there, his deep interest in music led him to pursue music studies at Jacksonville University with Gary Starling, head of the guitar department.

Bill then decided to move to Los Angeles to study at the Guitar Institute of Technology (GIT). Working his way through school as a pit orchestra player, Bill studied all types of music from rock, pop, and funk to Latin, Cuban, fusion, and jazz. Dedicated and driven to learn all GIT had to teach in music, Bill graduated with honors. Ready to move to New York City to start his career, Bill changed his plans when Steve Freeman, President of Atlanta Institute of Music (AIM), called him and offered him a position as guitar instructor at his school in Atlanta, Georgia.

Bill began teaching at AIM and is now the head of the guitar department. He has done seminars with some of music's finest players, such as Peter Erskine, Chuck Silverman, Robbin Dimagio, Jimmy Herring (Aquarium Rescue Unit), and Shane Theriot (Neville Brothers guitarist). He has played on several recording sessions for Atlanta-based producers Randy Hoexter, Huston Singletary, and Tom Kidd. He is the guitarist for the recording group Liquid Blue, who have opened for Mike Stern, Dave Weckl, Lou Rawls, Joey DeFrancesco, Acoustic Alchemy, and the Yellow Jackets (Jacksonville Jazz Festival).

Bill continues to study music with jazz legends Mike Stern, Steve Khan, Scott Henderson, and Wayne Krantz. As an instructor, he knows that continued study enhances your playing, teaching, composition, and your growth as a musician.

Studying and playing guitar for 25 years, Bill Hart's music is a compilation of the many styles he enjoys. His current vision is to continue recording and tour as a side man with a major recording group. He can be contacted at:

Atlanta Institute of Music
C/O Bill Hart
6145-D Northbelt Parkway
Norcross, GA 30071-2972
email: canuck@mindspring.com

INTRODUCTION

I have taught guitar at the Atlanta Institute of Music for the last 10 years, where one of my master classes focuses on the study of chord melody. Through this course, I have found that studying chord melody and reharmonizing tunes is one of the strongest music-learning experiences available. I have taught students from all over the world, with interests in all styles of music, and have seen them all benefit from studying chord melody.

The first eleven units cover a variety of chord melody techniques with an explanation of each one. The first step is to study each technique extensively. Units 12 through 31 then use a combination of these techniques in twenty familiar jazz standards. One of the analogies I use in my master jazz class to help students understand the concept of improvising is to compare soloing and reharmonizing tunes to making a cake. A cake has several ingredients, one being salt. Making a cake with nothing but salt would be the same as reharmonizing or soloing with only one concept. Feel free to take the liberty to enhance any of the techniques in the songs. For example, if you have a chord on a quarter note with three quarter notes following, try voicing the chord to play through the whole measure, giving you the harmony with the melody over it. Some other examples would be to try using false harmonics as the melody or to play single bass notes with the melody on top to create implied harmony. Jazz is wide open; the main rule to follow is: if your ear likes it, it's right.

CHORD MELODY CONCEPTS
DIATONIC SUBSTITUTION

Diatonic substitutions occur when chords in a harmonized scale are used to substitute for each other. The types of diatonic substitutions are:

- II subs for IV, and vice versa
- V subs for VII, and vice versa
- I, III, and VI chords are all interchangeable

Substituting II for IV and IV for II

Using Fmaj7 in place of Dm7 creates a Dm9 sound. Conversely, using Dm7 in place of Fmaj7 will create an F6 sound. In Fig. 1, we have a I–VI–II–V progression. Measure 3 uses Fmaj7 and Fmaj13 (the IV chord) to substitute for Dm7 (the II chord).

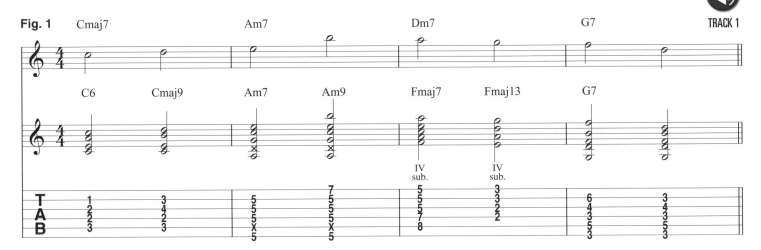

Substituting V for VII and VII for V

Using G7 in place of Bm7♭5 creates a Bm7♭5♯5 sound. Conversely, using Bm7♭5 in place of G7 will create a G9 sound. In Fig. 2, we again have a I–VI–II–V progression. The first half note in measure 3 uses Fmaj7 (the IV chord) to substitute for Dm7 (the II chord). In measure 4, the first half note is Bm7♭5 (the VII chord), substituting for G7 (the V chord), creating a G9 sound.

Substituting I, III, and VI interchangeably

Using Cmaj7 in place of Em7 creates a Em7♯5 sound. Conversely, using Em7 in place of Cmaj7 creates a first inversion of Cmaj7—or Cmaj7/E. Using Am7 in place of Cmaj7 creates a C6 sound. Conversely, using Cmaj7 in place of Am7 creates an Am9 sound. In Fig. 3, I've reharmonized the I–VI–II–V using Am7 and Em7 to sub for Cmaj7 (the I chord). In measure 2, I've substituted Cmaj7 and Em11 for Am7 (the VI chord). In measure 3, the first half note uses Fmaj7 (the IV chord) to substitute for Dm7 (the II chord). In measure 4, the first half note uses Bm7♭5 (the VII chord) to substitute for G7 (the V chord), creating a G9 sound.

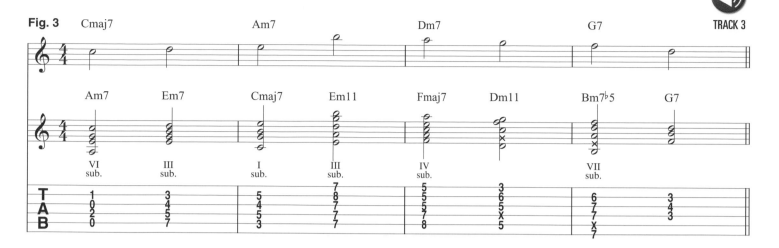

Fig. 3

TRACK 3

MINOR THIRD SUBSTITUTION

A *minor 3rd substitution* takes either the II chord, the V chord, or both the II and V up or down a minor 3rd before resolving to I.

Fig. 4 has a II–V–I progression in G major. I substituted the II chord (Am7) up a minor 3rd to Cm7, then to D7 (the V chord), and finally to Gmaj7 (the I chord).

Fig. 4 – IIm7 Minor 3rd Substitution

TRACK 4

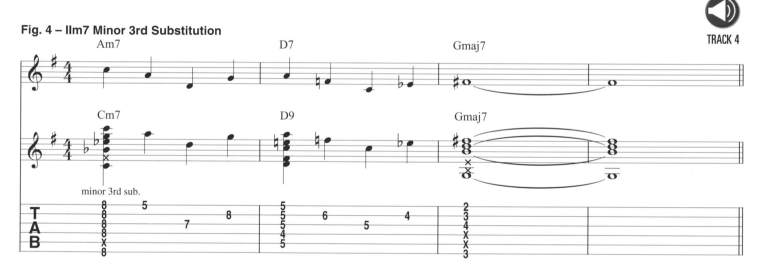

Fig. 5 has the same II–V–I progression in G major, only I've substituted F7 for D7 (the V chord), resolving to Gmaj7 (the I chord).

Fig. 5 – V7 Minor 3rd Substitution

TRACK 5

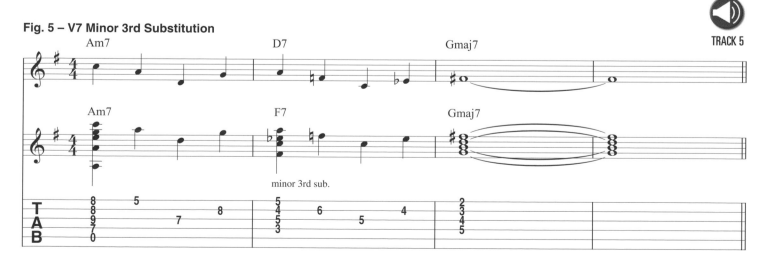

In Fig. 6, I've substituted the Am7 *and* D7 (the II–V) up a minor 3rd using Cm7 and F7, before resolving to Gmaj7 (the I chord).

Fig. 6 – IIm7 and V7 Minor 3rd Substitution

TRACK 6

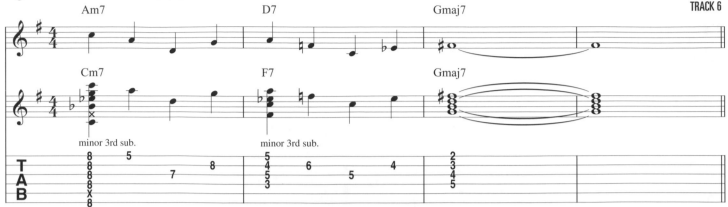

Play through these examples and let your ears be the judge. This is a very hip way to create some different sounds for a II–V–I progression. Remember: this concept is endless. By moving in minor 3rds, it creates somewhat of a diminished sound. You can experiment with soloing using the same concept. For example, play a II–V line over Cm7 and F7 and resolve it to Gmaj7.

CHORD-NOTE

Chord-note playing is just like it sounds: you hit a chord, followed by one, two, or three single melody notes.

A chord followed by three notes (chord-note-note-note) works well with uptempo tunes. Fig. 7 has a II–V–I progression using this concept.

Fig. 7 – Chord-Note-Note-Note

TRACK 7

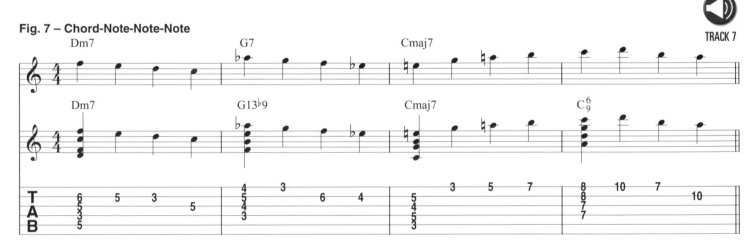

Playing a chord followed by two notes (chord-note-note) sounds best with tunes in 3/4. Fig. 8 has a I–VI–II–V progression in 3/4 using this concept. Try experimenting with this in a 4/4 time signature to create some interesting three-against-four-type feels.

Fig. 8 – Chord-Note-Note

TRACK 8

Alternating between chords and single notes (chord-note) works well with a tune that has a lot of melody notes at a slower tempo. Fig. 9 has a II–V–I progression using this concept.

Fig. 9 – Chord-Note

TRACK 9

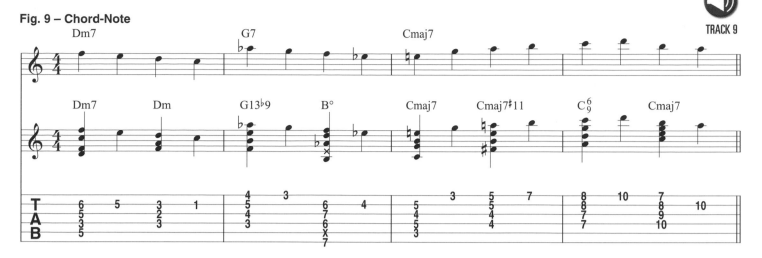

BACK CYCLING

The key to *back cycling* is imagining the chord you will be resolving to and counting backwards via the V chord.

In Fig. 10, I have a II–V–I in C major. I start at C and work my way backwards to put a chord over each note. G7 is the V of C and Dm7 is the II chord. A7 is called V/II and Em7 is the II/V/II. You can use this concept with as many notes as you want depending on how busy you want the harmony.

Fig. 10 – Back Cycling from I

TRACK 10

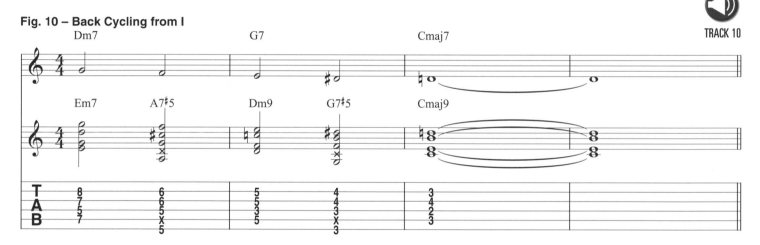

Fig. 11 is exactly the same as Fig. 10, except I replaced the dominant chord with a tritone substitution. The D♭9 in measure 2 is subbing for G7, and the E♭9 in measure 1 is subbing for A7. Another concept to experiment with would be changing the minor chords to dominant chords, creating chromatic harmony similar to a big band sound.

Fig. 11 – Back Cycling with Tritone Substitutions

TRACK 11

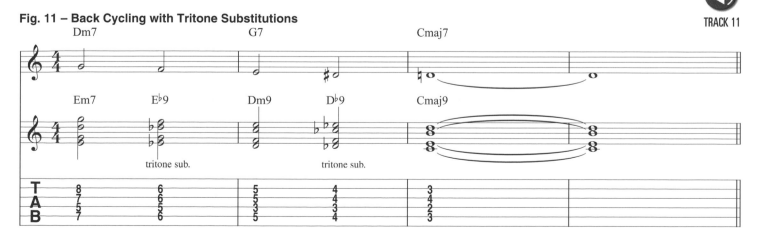

Fig. 12 is the same as Fig. 11, except the dominant chords have all been changed to maj7 chords, creating a softer sound and resolution to I.

Fig. 12 – Back Cycling with Maj7 Tritone Substitutions (Softer Sound)

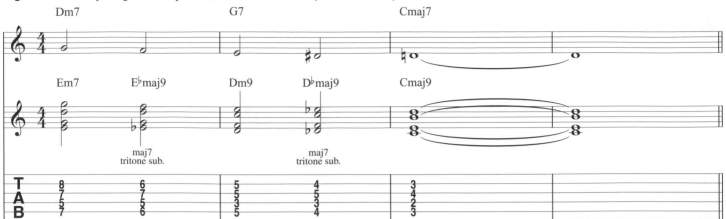

THE V CHORD

The V chord concept we'll examine takes the Ionian, Dorian, or Mixolydian scale and places the V chord on every other note. The V chord can always resolve to I, giving tension in the scale and releasing back to the chord used in the scale or mode.

Fig. 13 is the C Ionian scale, better known as the C major scale. The first chord is C6, starting with C on top; the next melody note is D, which is the 5th of a G7; the next note is E, the 3rd of Cmaj7; next is F, the ♭7 of G7; then G, the 5th of C6/9; the next note, A, is the 9th of G7; then there's B, which is the 7th of Cmaj7. The next note is C—only this time we have a G7 chord instead of Cmaj7. With C as the melody note, this gives us G11. The next note is D, the 9th of Cmaj7; the next note is E, the 13th of G; the next note is F♯: over a maj7 chord we have to raise the 4th a half step (F to F♯), creating Lydian. (An F♮ over a Cmaj7 chord sounds ugly. On a G7, the F note is the ♭7, and resolves to Cmaj7.) The last note is G, the root of a G9 chord.

Fig. 13 – V7 of Ionian (Major)

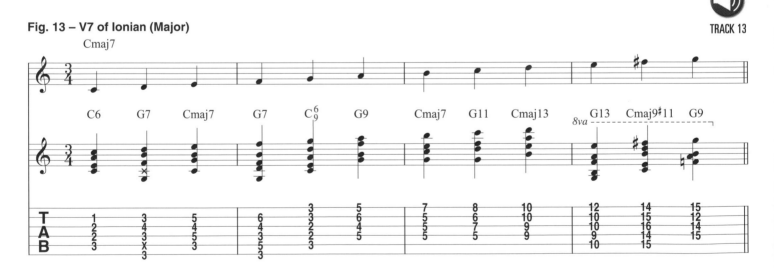

Figs. 14 and 15 use the exact same concept as Fig. 13, except the Dorian scale is used in Fig. 14 and the Mixolydian scale is used in Fig. 15.

Fig. 14 – V7 of Dorian

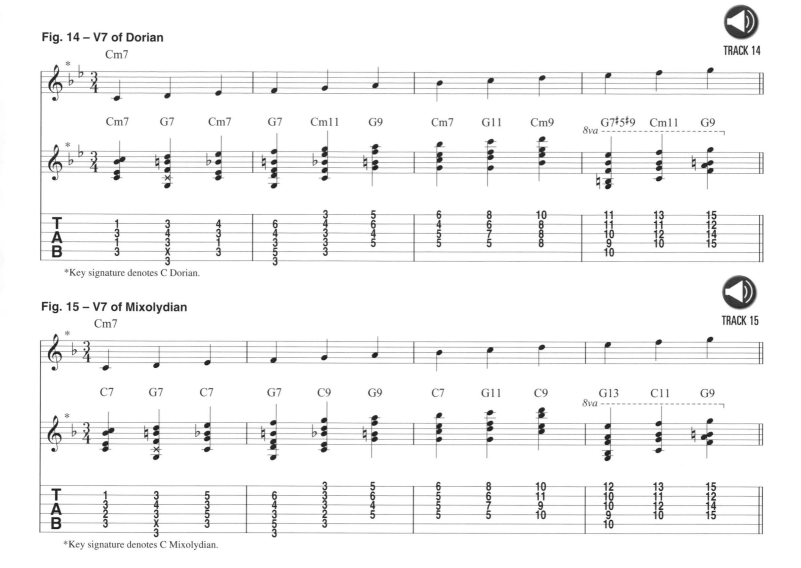

*Key signature denotes C Dorian.

Fig. 15 – V7 of Mixolydian

*Key signature denotes C Mixolydian.

CHORD SCALES WITH TENSION

Figs. 16 and 17 use chord scales harmonizing C6 and Cm6, respectively. In these figures, the V chord is again alternated with the I—in this case creating a 7♭9 sound. A diminished chord is the same as a 7♭9 chord with no root (D°7 = G7♭9 without the root). The 7♭9 chord creates a lot more tension, strongly wanting to resolve to I.

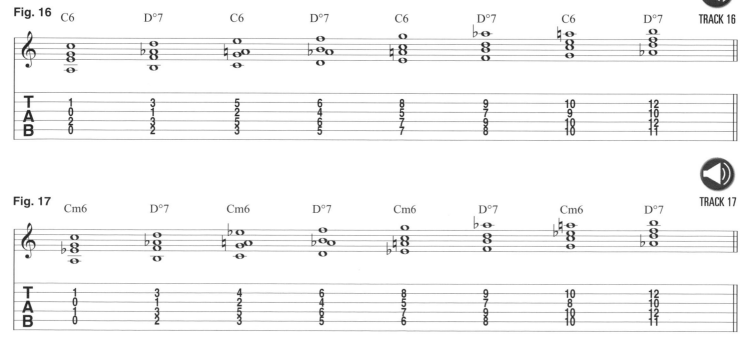

Fig. 16

Fig. 17

MODAL CHORD SCALES

There are seven notes in a scale, four of which make up a corresponding seventh chord (maj7, m7, or dom7 depending on the scale). The three remaining notes of the scale are embellished tones—the 9th, 11th, and 13th. When seeing the symbol m7 and dom7, you can take the liberty of adding the 9th, 11th, or 13th. On maj7 chords, you can add the 9th, #11th, and 13th. Fig. 18 uses C Lydian, Fig. 19 uses C Dorian, and Fig. 20 uses C Mixolydian. Practice playing up and down these scales just as you would sequencing an exercise. This will help you learn many voicings of the same quality all over the guitar neck.

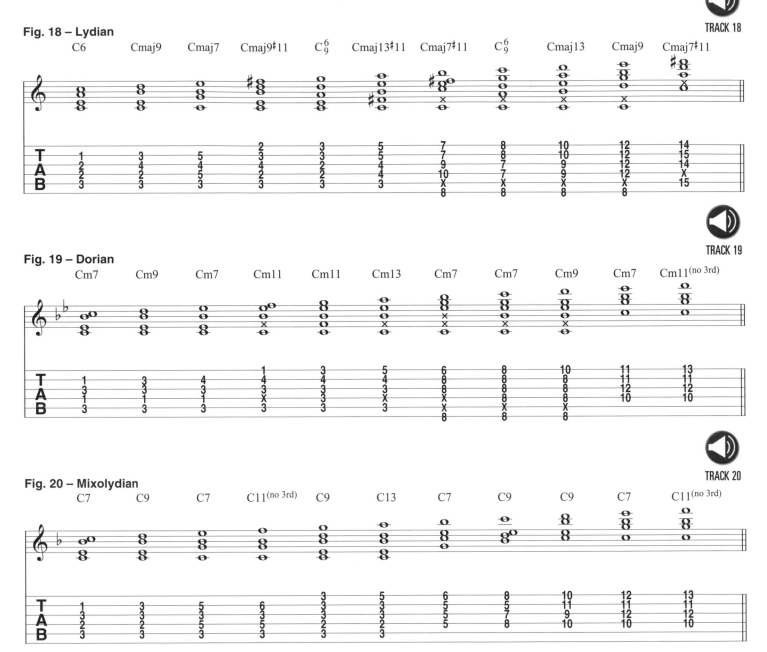

ASCENDING AND DESCENDING BASS HARMONY

Ascending/descending bass harmony uses three qualities of chords: major, minor, and dominant. This concept is much like back cycling. The difference is that you can approach your key chord from above or below. All examples use a II–V–I in Cmaj7. The II and the V are the chords that will be reharmonized on the way to Cmaj7. First, count how many melody notes there are, which indicates how many bass notes will be used. For example, there are four melody notes before Cmaj7, so four bass notes can be played, chromatically ascending, that resolve to Cmaj7. The next step is to harmonize the bass with the melody. I have given three examples using dominant, minor, and major. Generally, try to stay with one quality—meaning that if you decide to use dominant, use this until you resolve to the I chord (melody permitting).

Harmonizing the bass and the melody

The first melody note is E, and the bass note is A♭—a ♯5 interval. The second melody note is C and the bass note is A, creating a minor 3rd (or ♯9) interval. If I were using maj7, I could still use the minor 3rd by creating a m(maj7) chord. The third melody note is G with B♭ in the bass, which creates a 6th or 13th sound. The fourth melody note is F with B in the bass, creating a ♭5 sound resolving to Cmaj7. The figures show what the chord quality would be using maj7, min7, and dom7.

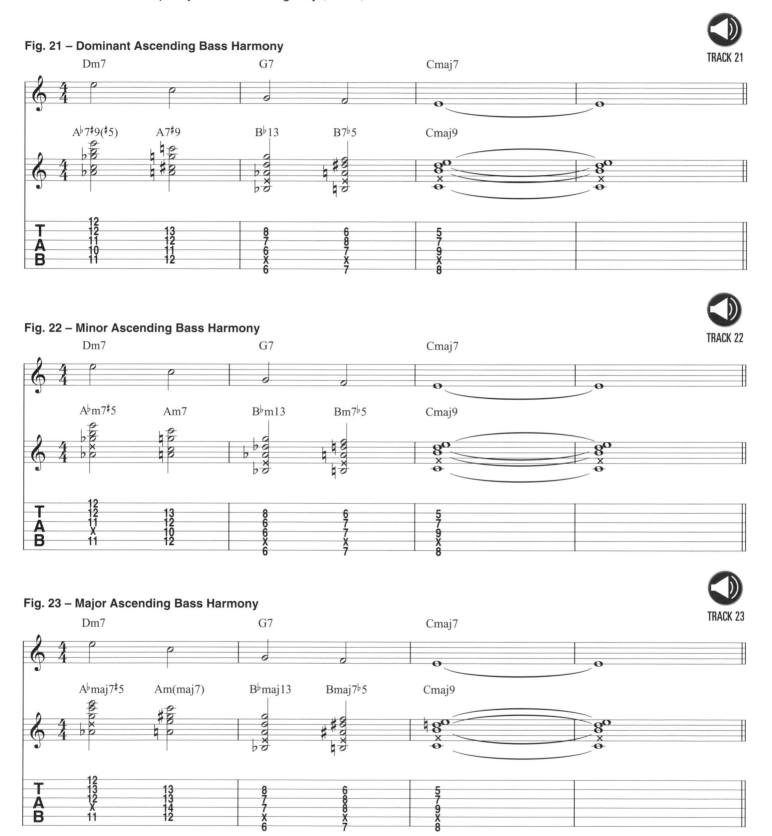

Fig. 21 – Dominant Ascending Bass Harmony

TRACK 21

Fig. 22 – Minor Ascending Bass Harmony

TRACK 22

Fig. 23 – Major Ascending Bass Harmony

TRACK 23

Descending bass harmony works exactly the same way as ascending bass harmony except that the bass will obviously be descending. Try experimenting with ascending and descending bass lines, but really use your ears because some of these will fall in the pocket and some will not work at all—your ears will tell you which ones work.

Fig. 24 – Dominant Descending Bass Harmony

TRACK 24

Fig. 25 – Minor Descending Bass Harmony

TRACK 25

Fig. 26– Major Descending Bass Harmony

TRACK 26

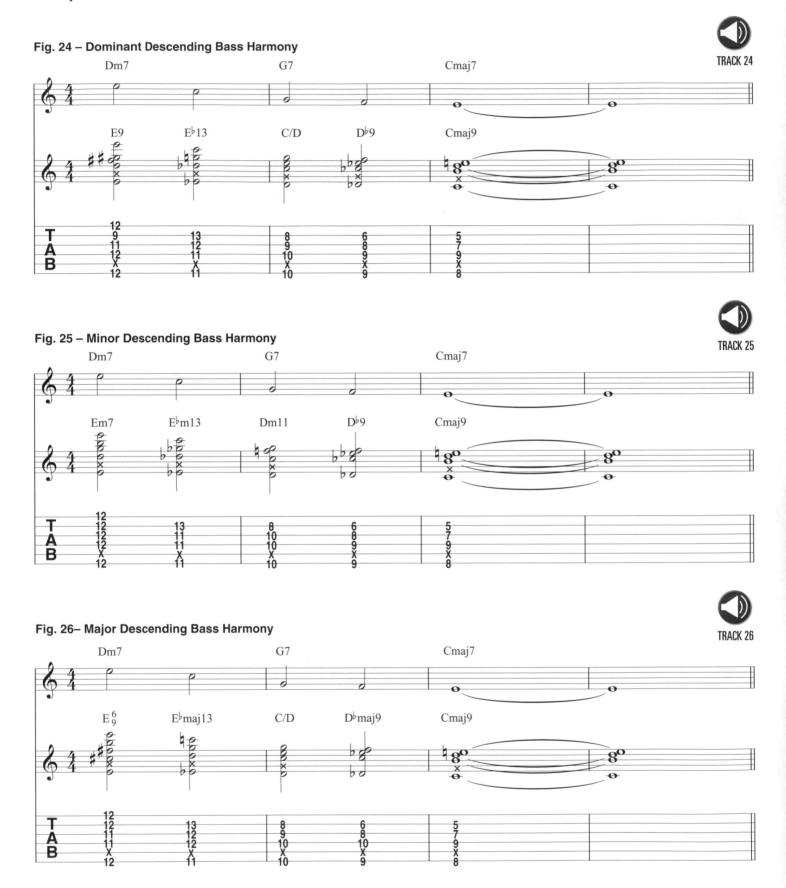

CONTRARY MOTION

Contrary motion is like ascending or descending bass harmony, except that the melody and bass line move in contrary motion (in opposite directions). You take the same concept that applies to ascending and descending bass harmony—harmonizing the bass with the melody—but the direction of the melody will dictate the direction of the bass movement.

In Fig. 27, the melody is ascending, and the bass is descending. In Fig. 28, the melody is descending, and the bass is ascending. Fig. 29 contains a mixture of both, and may be a little more challenging.

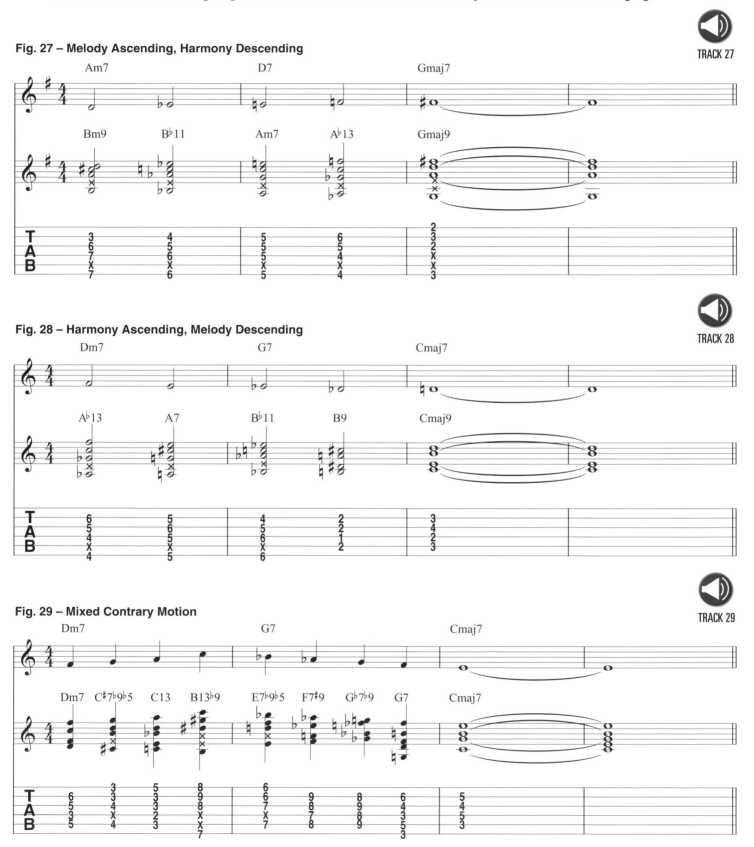

Fig. 27 – Melody Ascending, Harmony Descending

TRACK 27

Fig. 28 – Harmony Ascending, Melody Descending

TRACK 28

Fig. 29 – Mixed Contrary Motion

TRACK 29

WALKING BASS LINES

Walking bass lines are an essential part of playing chord melody. They will create the sound of another player walking underneath your harmonies and melodies. The strong beats are on 1 and 3, and the weak beats, or backbeats, are on 2 and 4. On the downbeats of 1 and 3, use the bass note on 1, then the harmony on the last eighth note of a triplet. The triplet is what makes it swing. On the backbeat, approach the target chord from either a half step above or below.

The following figures use a I–VI–II–V progression. Fig. 30 approaches each chord from a half step above. Fig. 31 approaches each chord from a half step below. Fig. 32 is a combination, approaching Cmaj7 from below, Am7 from above, Dm7 from below, and G7 from above. Fig. 33 approaches Cmaj7 from above, Am7 from below, Dm7 from above, and G7 from below.

Walking Bass Lines in F Blues

This is an example of walking a bass line through an F blues using a chord-note-note-note approach, with the note being the bass note. The exception to this is when there are two chords in one measure, you would use chord-note-chord-note.

Fig. 34 – F Blues with Walking Bass Line

TRACK 34

LINES IN THE SPACES

Lines in the spaces works well with a tune that uses a lot of half notes and whole notes, giving you a lot of space. You can fill in the spaces with lines to create more movement in the tune.

Fig. 35 is a II–V–I in C major, where the melody note is a whole note tied to a half note in measures 1 and 2. Here, the first melody note is played as a half note and filled in with a sixteenth-note line that corresponds with the chord qualities, and resolves into the melody notes.

TRACK 35

Fig. 35 – C Major "Lines in the Spaces"

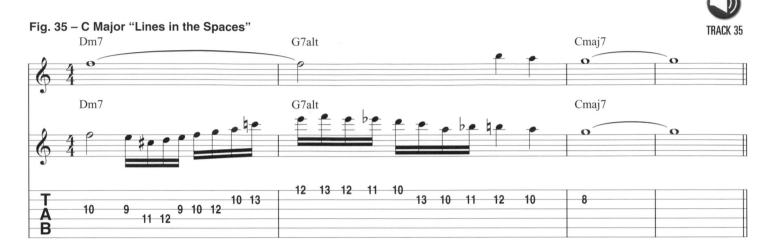

Fig. 36 is a II–V–I in G major. Here is an eighth-note line over the II chord and the V chord. The last beat of measure 2 is where the melody returns with two eighth notes.

TRACK 36

Fig. 36 – G Major "Lines in the Spaces"

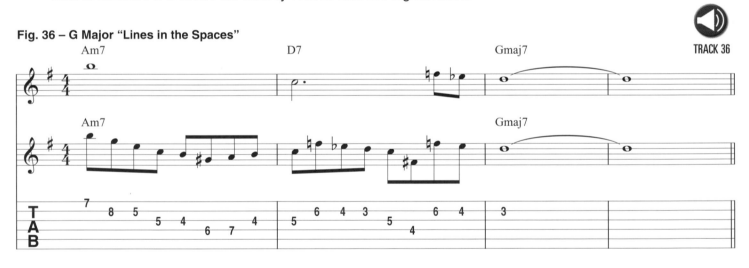

Fig. 37 is a II–V–I in E♭ major. Here the melody is played as written until the I chord, where rhythmic variations in the last half of measure 3 and all of measure 4 lead back to the A♭ melody note in measure 1.

TRACK 37

Fig. 37 – E♭ Major "Lines in the Spaces"

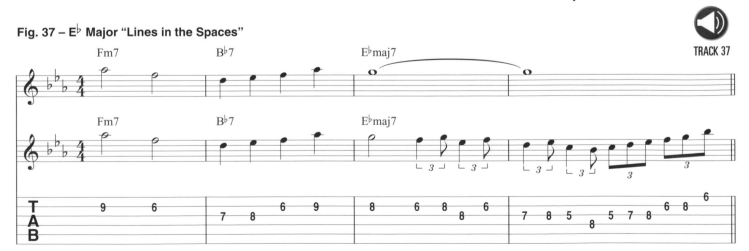

CHORD MELODY SONGS

TRACK 38

ALL THE THINGS YOU ARE

from *VERY WARM FOR MAY*

Lyrics by OSCAR HAMMERSTEIN II
Music by JEROME KERN

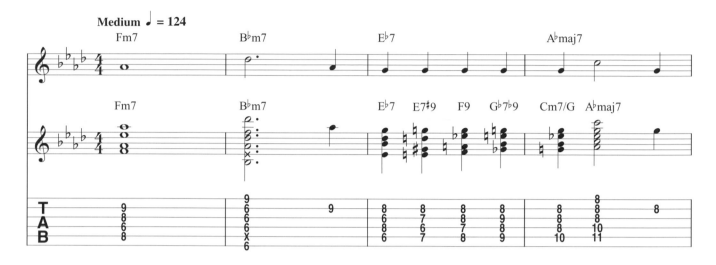

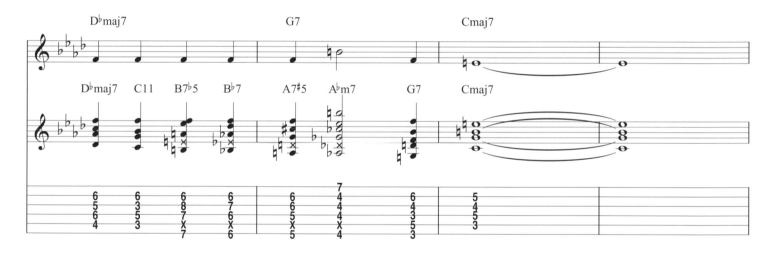

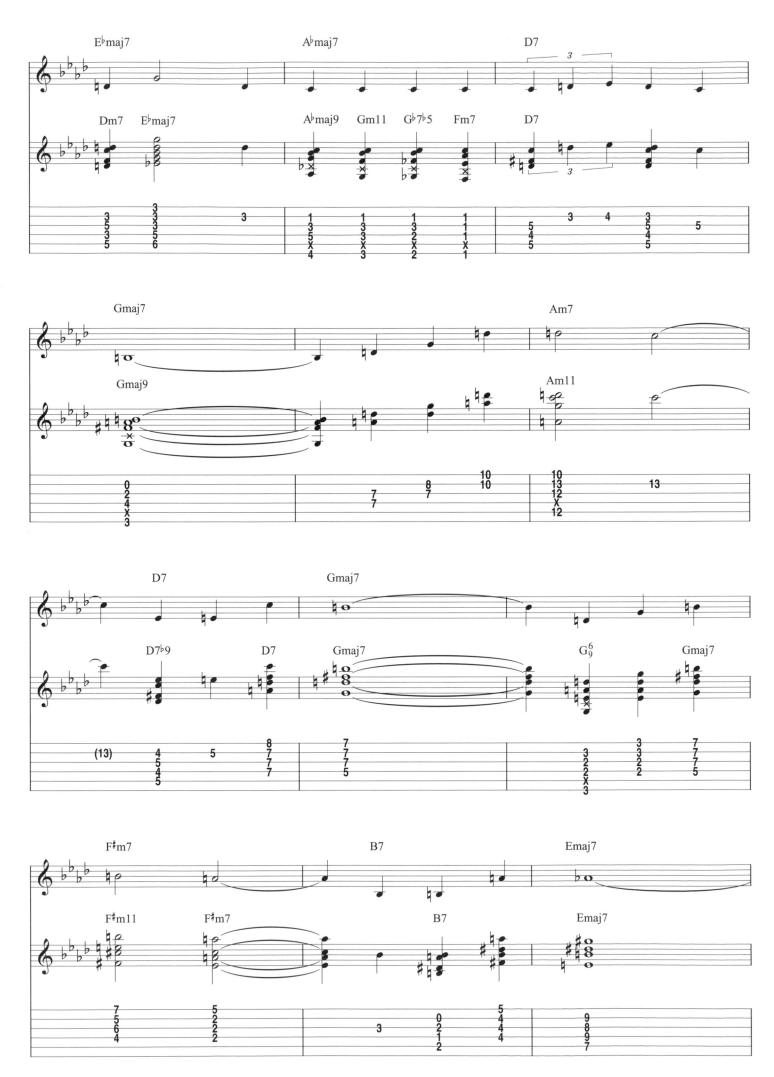

BLUE IN GREEN

By MILES DAVIS

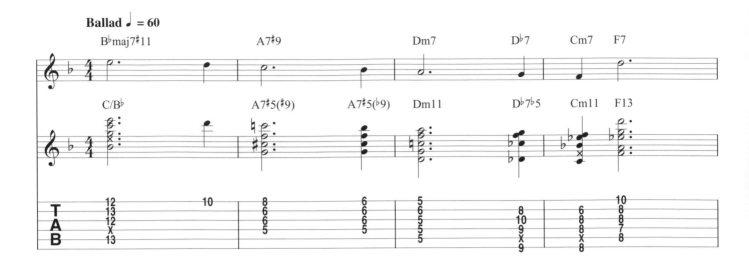

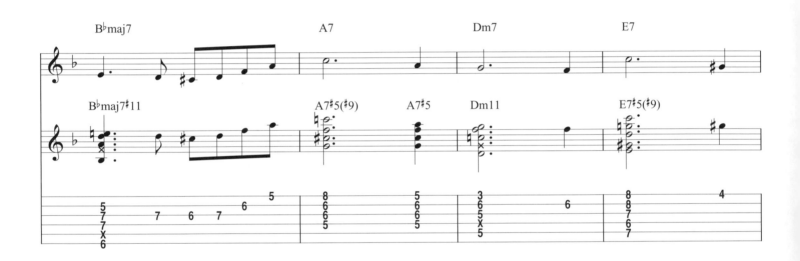

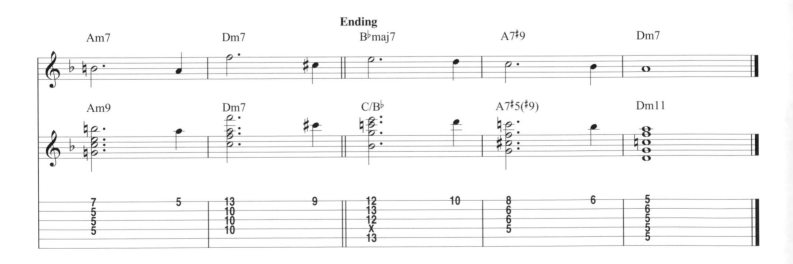

BLUESETTE

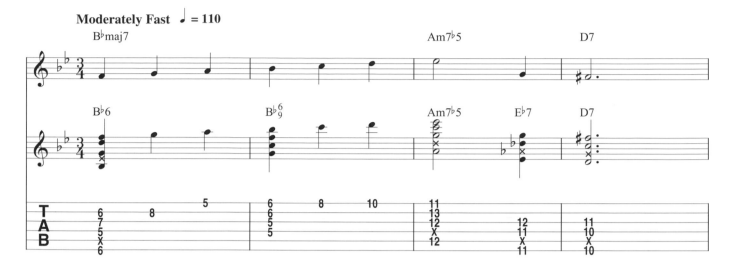

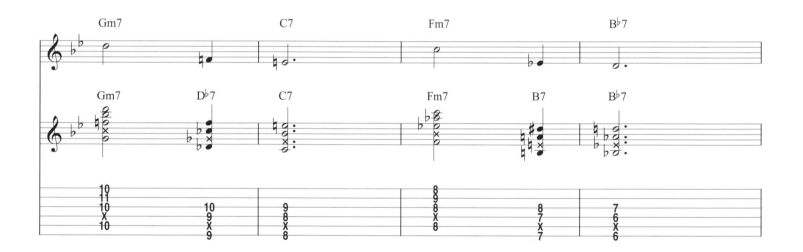

24

CHEROKEE
(Indian Love Song)

Words and Music by RAY NOBLE

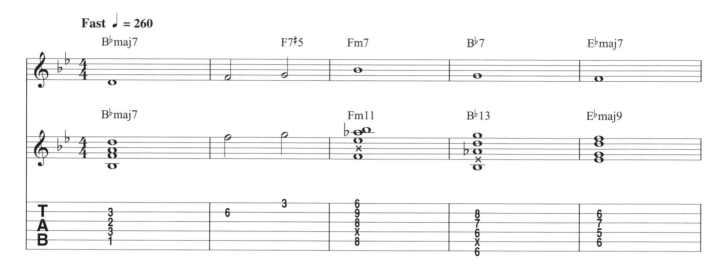

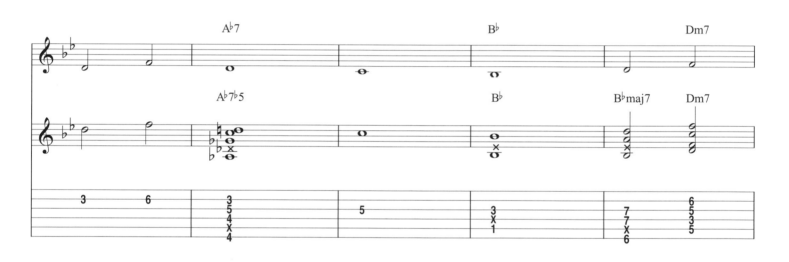

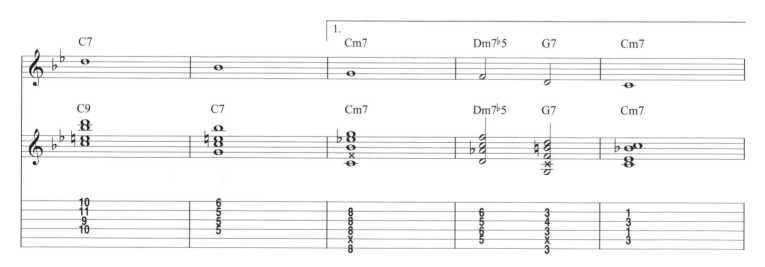

500 MILES HIGH

TRACK 42

Lyric by NEVILLE POTTER
Music by CHICK COREA

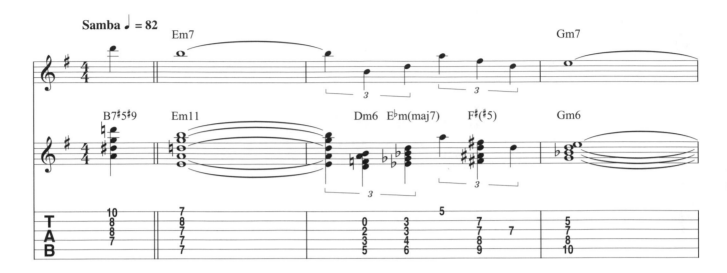

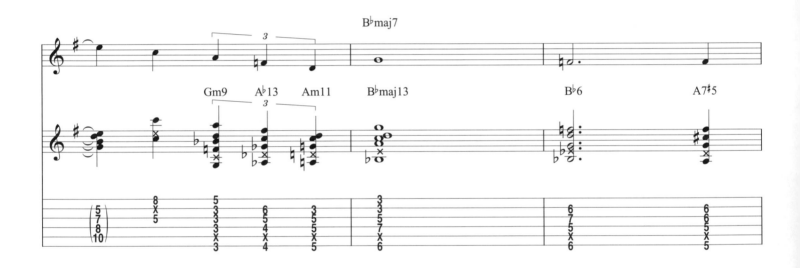

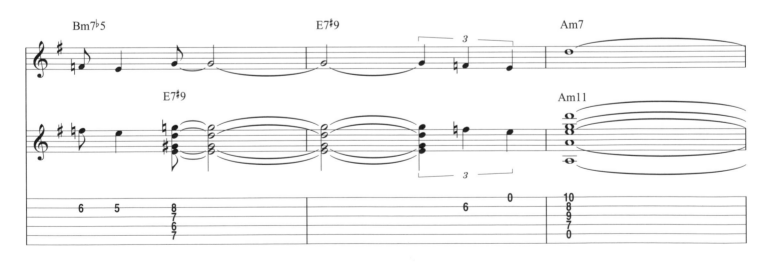

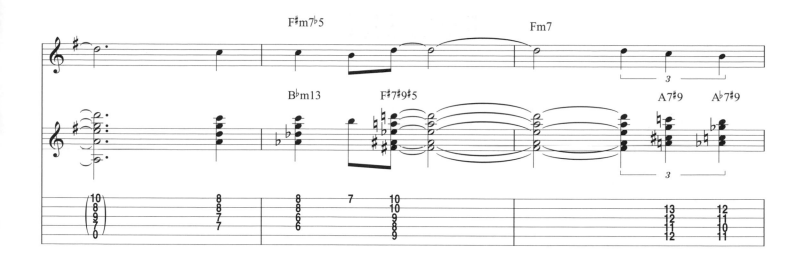

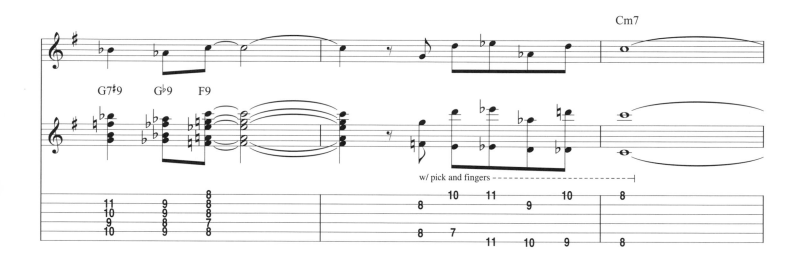

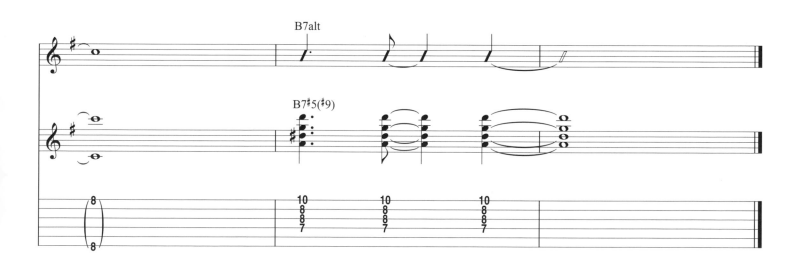

GIANT STEPS

By JOHN COLTRANE

HERE'S THAT RAINY DAY

from *CARNIVAL IN FLANDERS*

Words by JOHNNY BURKE
Music by JIMMY VAN HEUSEN

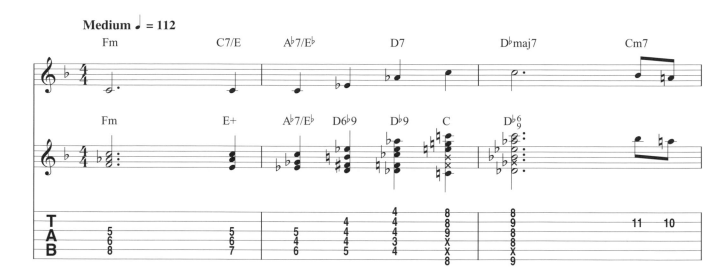

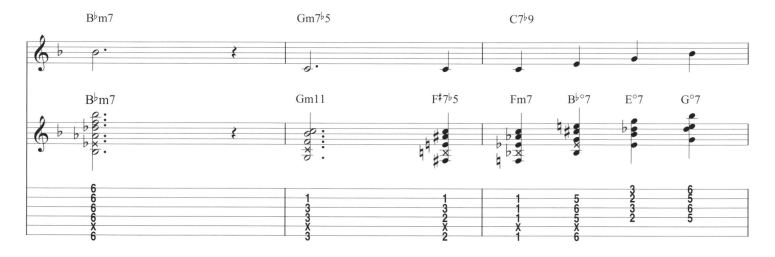

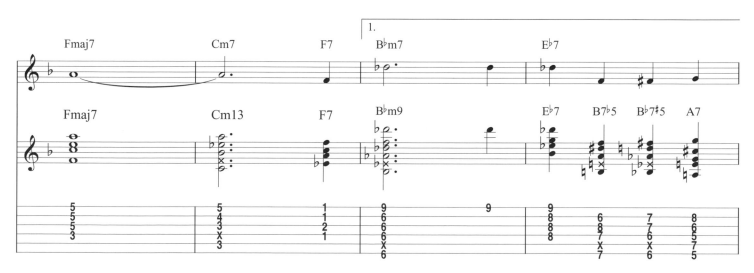

HOW INSENSITIVE
(Insensatez)

TRACK 45

Music by ANTONIO CARLOS JOBIM
Original Words by VINICIUS DE MORAES
English Words by NORMAN GIMBEL

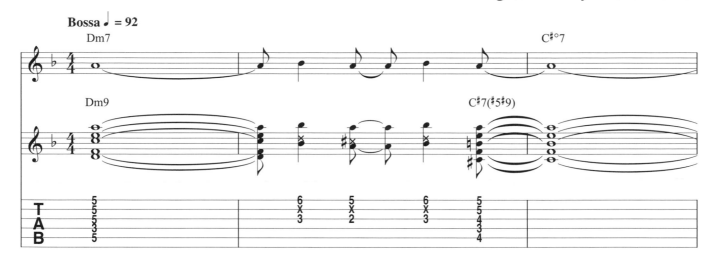

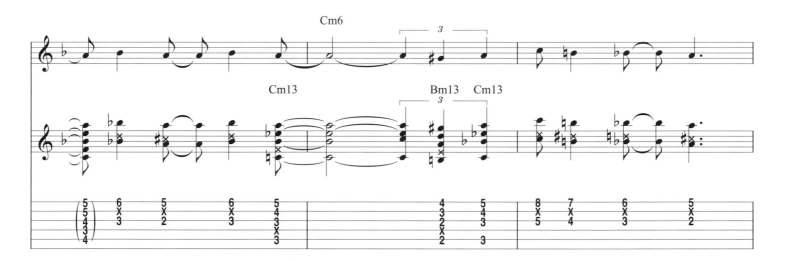

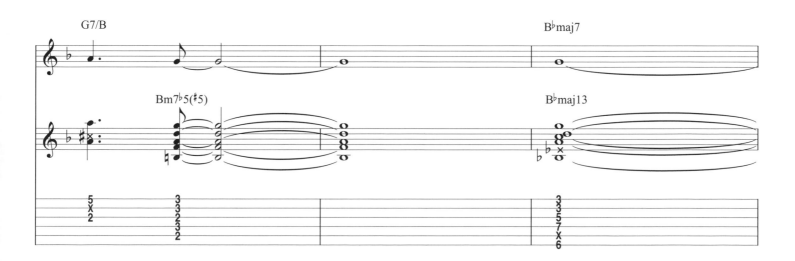

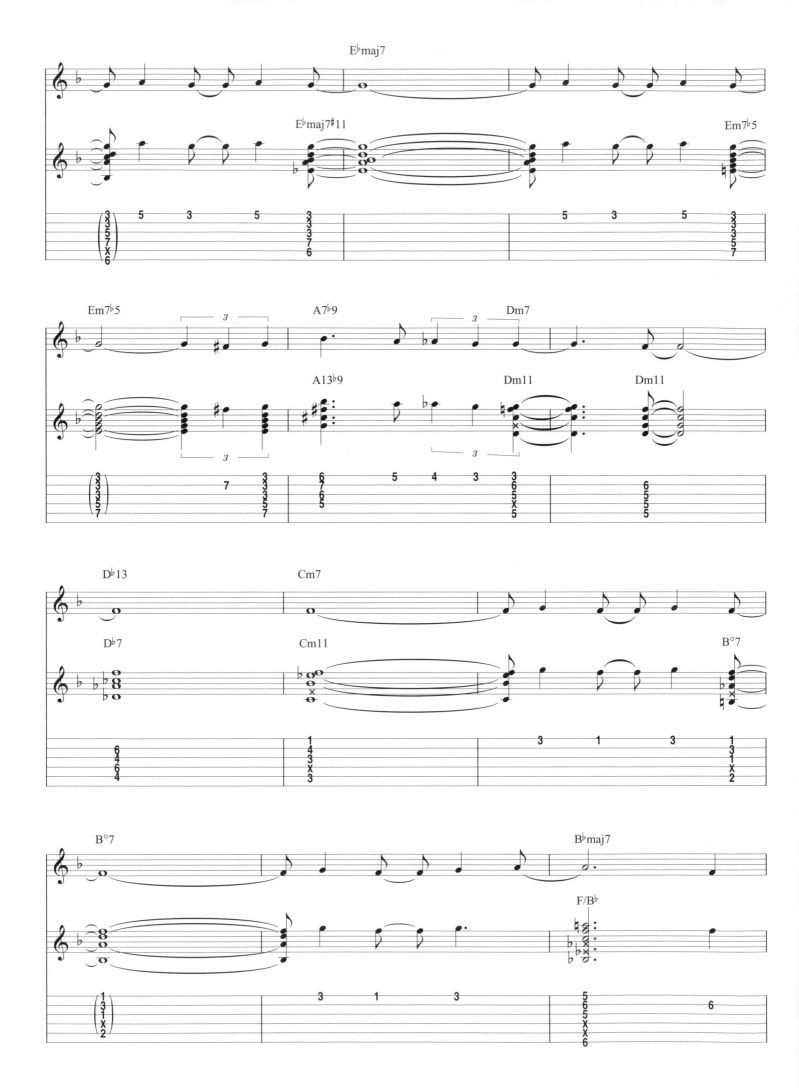

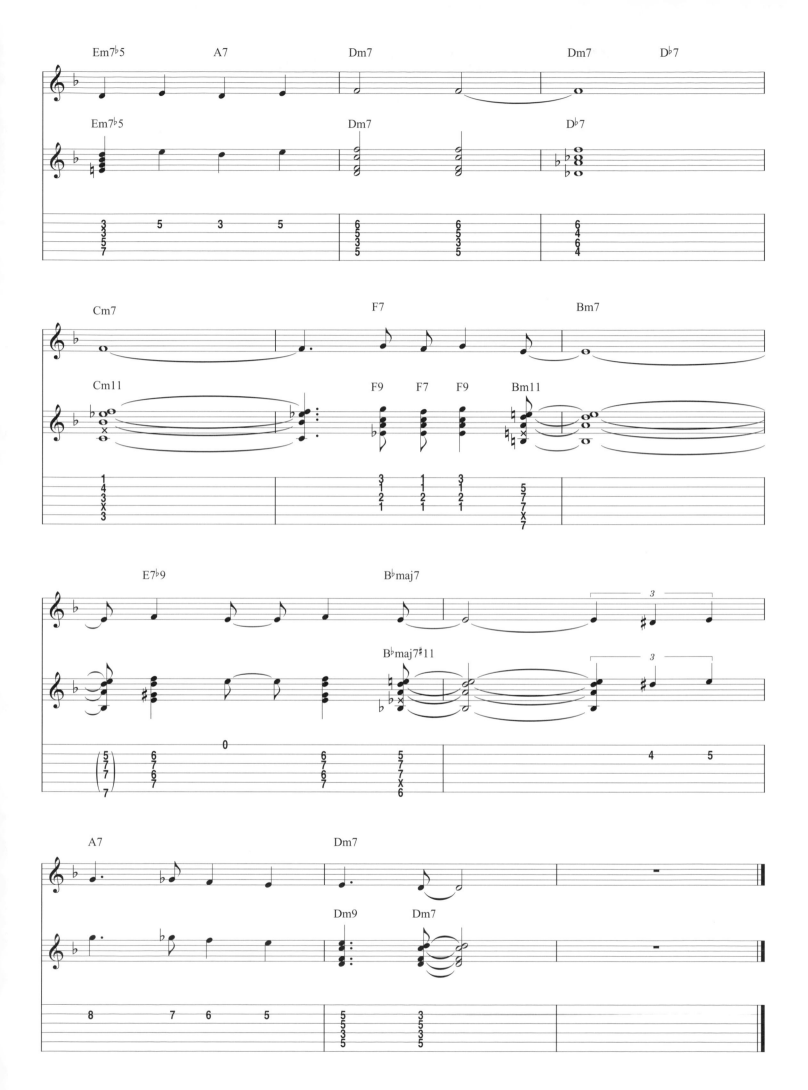

I COULD WRITE A BOOK

TRACK 46

from *PAL JOEY*

Words by LORENZ HART
Music by RICHARD RODGERS

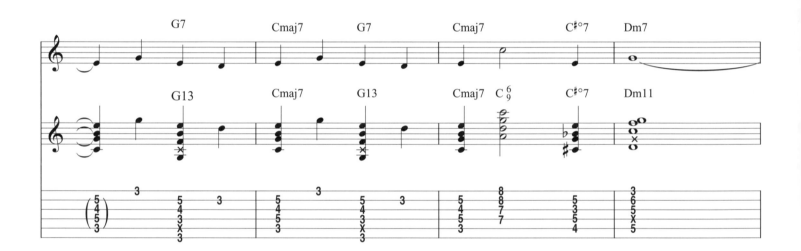

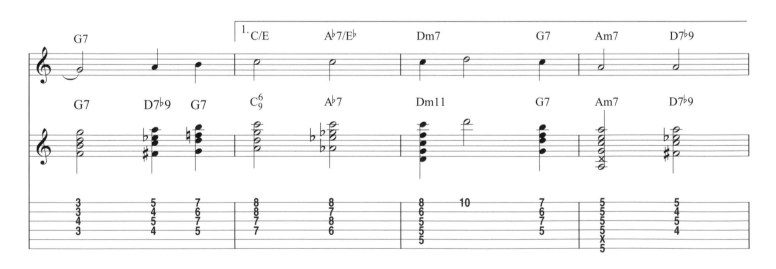

IN A SENTIMENTAL MOOD

By DUKE ELLINGTON

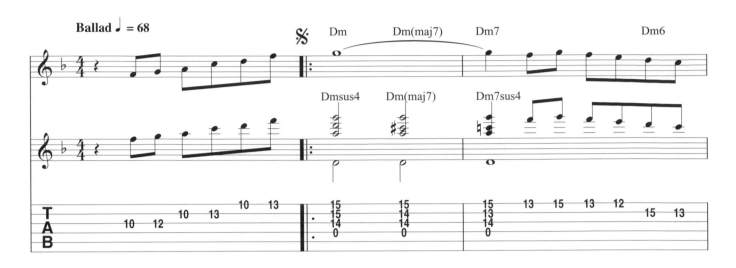

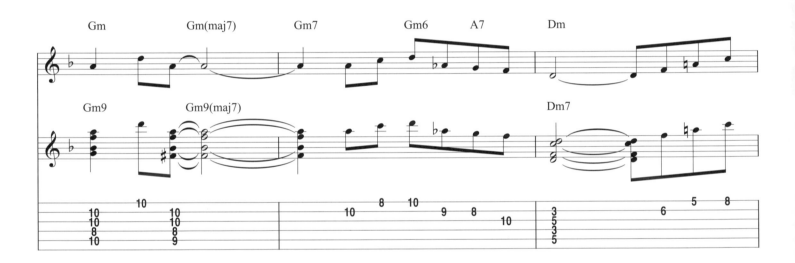

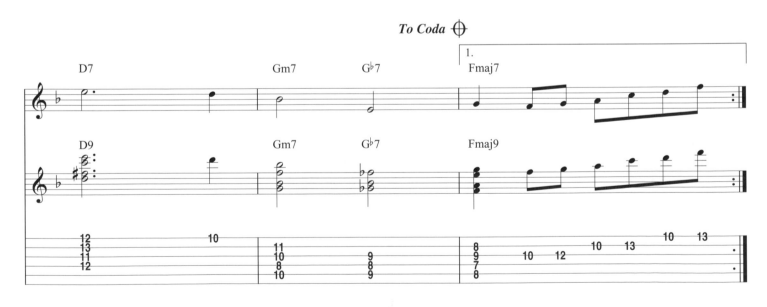

LIKE SOMEONE IN LOVE

Words by JOHNNY BURKE
Music by JIMMY VAN HEUSEN

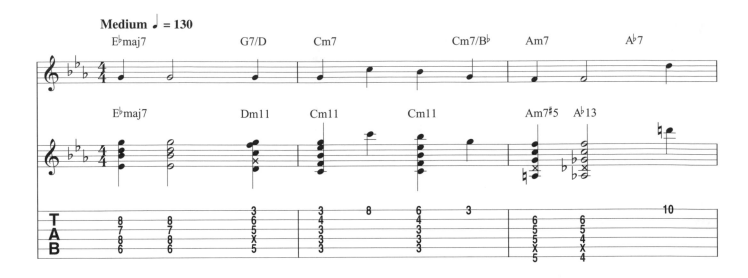

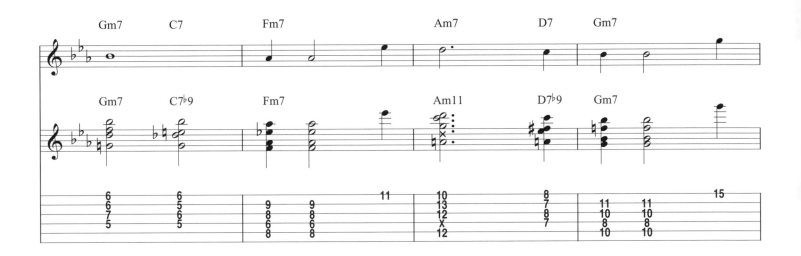

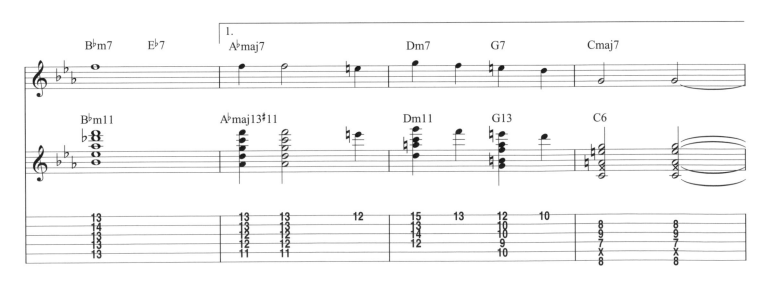

MY FAVORITE THINGS
from *THE SOUND OF MUSIC*

Lyrics by OSCAR HAMMERSTEIN II
Music by RICHARD RODGERS

*Fermata on Fine only.

MY FUNNY VALENTINE

from *BABES IN ARMS*

Lyrics by LORENZ HART
Music by RICHARD RODGERS

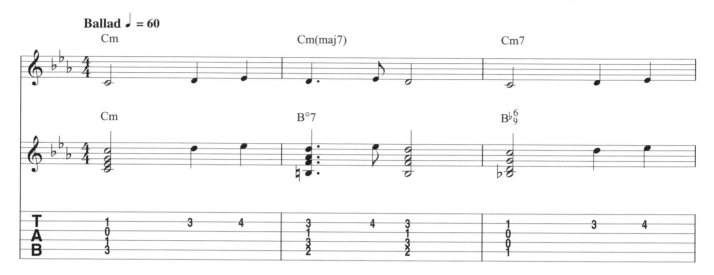

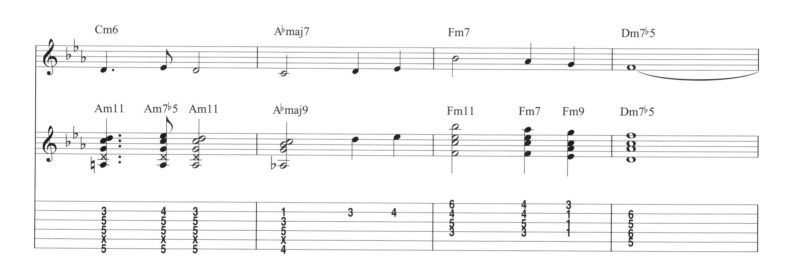

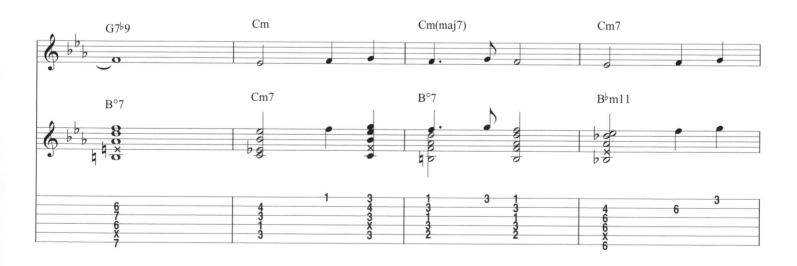

MY ONE AND ONLY LOVE

TRACK 51

Words by ROBERT MELLIN
Music by GUY WOOD

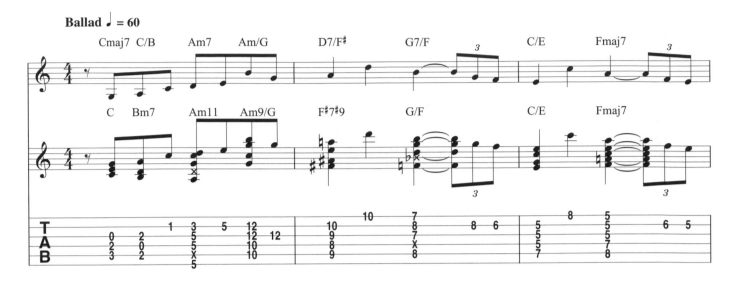

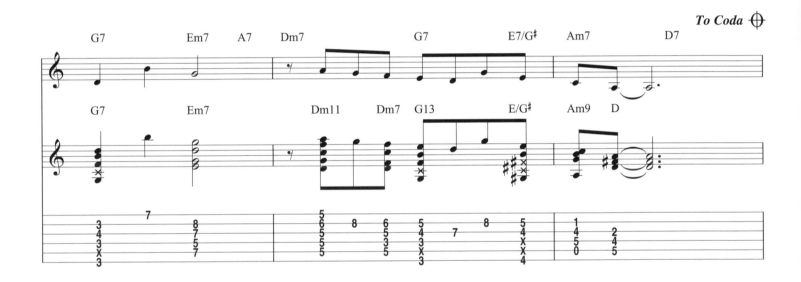

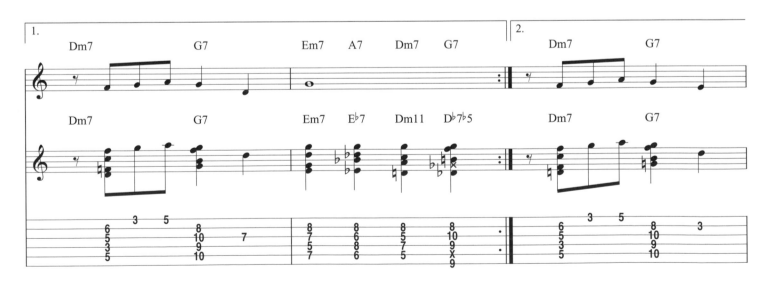

MY ROMANCE

from *JUMBO*

TRACK 52

Words by LORENZ HART
Music by RICHARD RODGERS

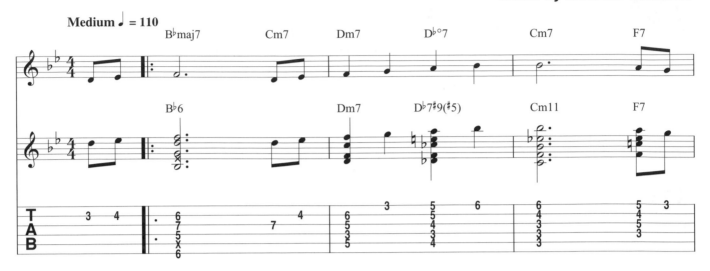

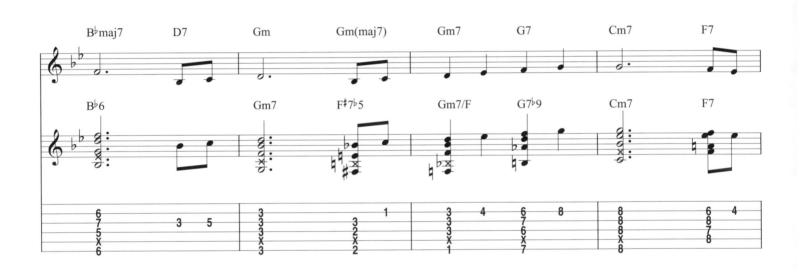

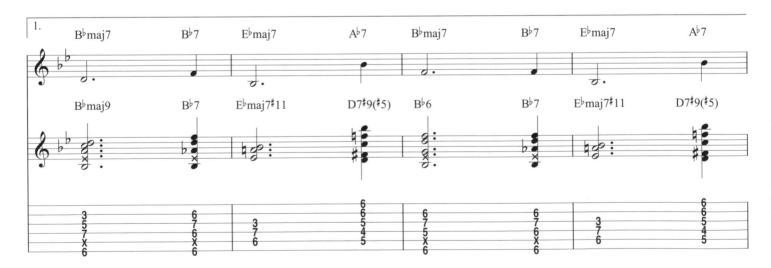

TRACK 53

STELLA BY STARLIGHT
from the Paramount Picture *THE UNINVITED*

Words by NED WASHINGTON
Music by VICTOR YOUNG

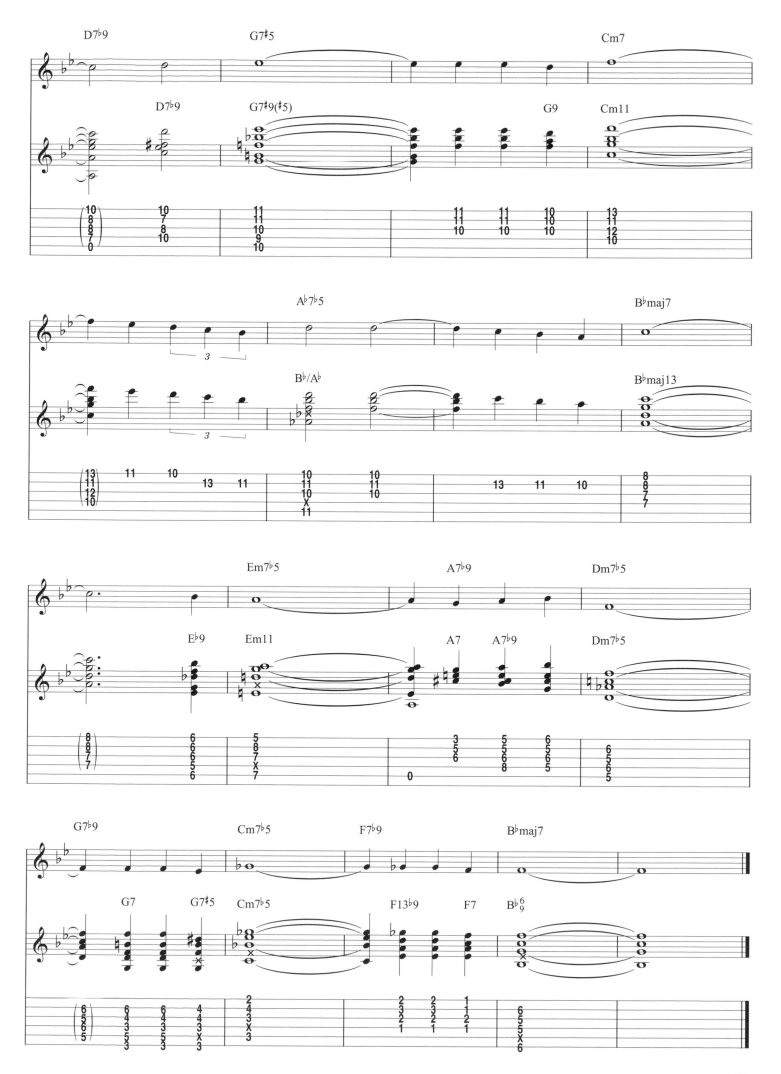

THERE IS NO GREATER LOVE

TRACK 54

Words by MARTY SYMES
Music by ISHAM JONES

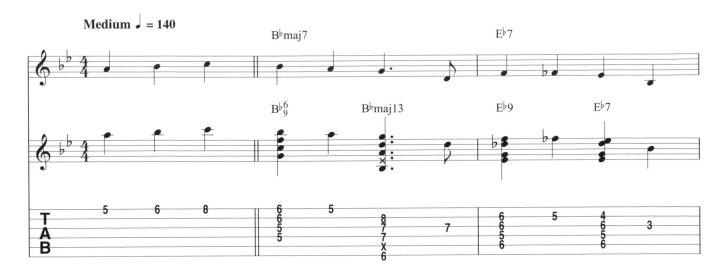

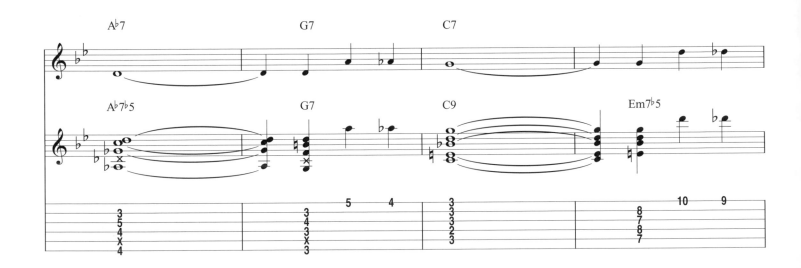

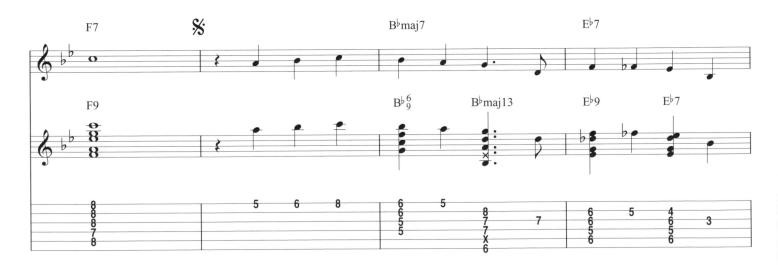

THERE WILL NEVER BE ANOTHER YOU

from the Motion Picture *ICELAND*

Lyric by MACK GORDON
Music by HARRY WARREN

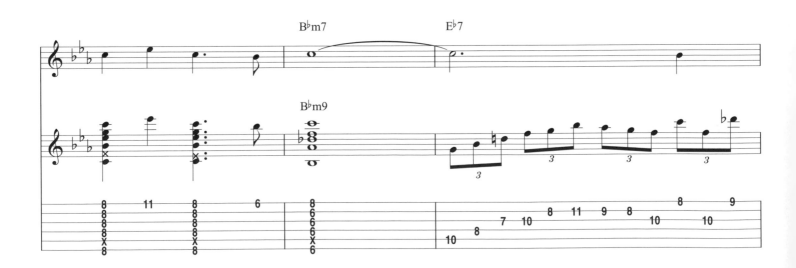

WINDOWS

TRACK 56

By CHICK COREA

Moderately Fast ♩ = 128

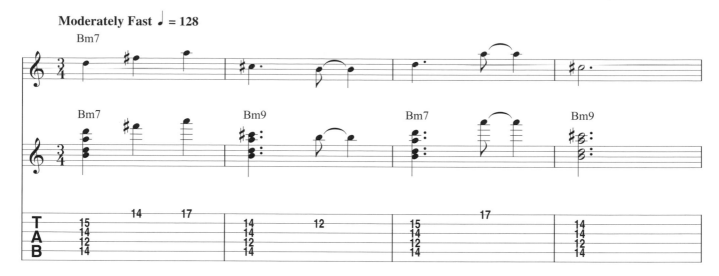

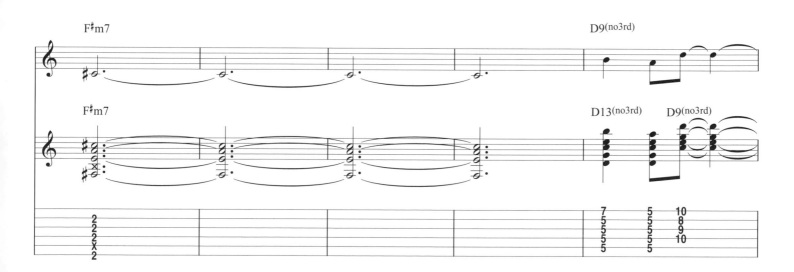

YESTERDAYS

from *ROBERTA*
from *LOVELY TO LOOK AT*

TRACK 57

Words by OTTO HARBACH
Music by JEROME KERN

ARTIST TRANSCRIPTIONS®

Artist Transcriptions are authentic, note-for-note transcriptions of today's hottest artists in jazz, pop and rock. These outstanding, accurate arrangements are in an easy-to-read format which includes all essential lines. Artist Transcriptions can be used to perform, sequence or for reference.

CLARINET
00672423	Buddy De Franco Collection	$19.95

FLUTE
00672379	Eric Dolphy Collection	$19.95
00672372	James Moody Collection – Sax and Flute	$19.95
00660108	James Newton – Improvising Flute	$14.95
00672455	Lew Tabackin Collection	$19.95

GUITAR & BASS
00660113	The Guitar Style of George Benson	$14.95
00672331	Ron Carter – Acoustic Bass	$16.95
00660115	Al Di Meola – Friday Night in San Francisco	$14.95
00604043	Al Di Meola – Music, Words, Pictures	$14.95
00673245	Jazz Style of Tal Farlow	$19.95
00672359	Bela Fleck and the Flecktones	$18.95
00699389	Jim Hall – Jazz Guitar Environments	$19.95
00699306	Jim Hall – Exploring Jazz Guitar	$19.95
00672335	Best of Scott Henderson	$24.95
00672356	Jazz Guitar Standards	$19.95
00675536	Wes Montgomery – Guitar Transcriptions	$17.95
00672353	Joe Pass Collection	$18.95
00673216	John Patitucci	$16.95
00672374	Johnny Smith Guitar Solos	$16.95
00672320	Mark Whitfield	$19.95
00672337	Gary Willis Collection	$19.95

PIANO & KEYBOARD
00672338	Monty Alexander Collection	$19.95
00672487	Monty Alexander Plays Standards	$19.95
00672318	Kenny Barron Collection	$22.95
00672520	Count Basie Collection	$19.95
00672364	Warren Bernhardt Collection	$19.95
00672439	Cyrus Chestnut Collection	$19.95
00673242	Billy Childs Collection	$19.95
00672300	Chick Corea – Paint the World	$12.95
00672537	Bill Evans at Town Hall	$16.95
00672425	Bill Evans – Piano Interpretations	$19.95
00672365	Bill Evans – Piano Standards	$19.95
00672510	Bill Evans Trio – Vol. 1: 1959-1961	$24.95
00672511	Bill Evans Trio – Vol. 2: 1962-1965	$24.95
00672512	Bill Evans Trio – Vol. 3: 1968-1974	$24.95
00672513	Bill Evans Trio – Vol. 4: 1979-1980	$24.95
00672329	Benny Green Collection	$19.95
00672486	Vince Guaraldi Collection	$19.95
00672419	Herbie Hancock Collection	$19.95
00672446	Gene Harris Collection	$19.95
00672438	Hampton Hawes	$19.95
00672322	Ahmad Jamal Collection	$22.95
00672476	Brad Mehldau Collection	$19.95

00672390	Thelonious Monk Plays Jazz Standards – Volume 1	$19.95
00672391	Thelonious Monk Plays Jazz Standards – Volume 2	$19.95
00672433	Jelly Roll Morton – The Piano Rolls	$12.95
00672542	Oscar Peterson – Jazz Piano Solos	$14.95
00672544	Oscar Peterson – Originals	$9.95
00672532	Oscar Peterson – Plays Broadway	$19.95
00672531	Oscar Peterson – Plays Duke Ellington	$19.95
00672533	Oscar Peterson – Trios	$24.95
00672543	Oscar Peterson Trio – Canadiana Suite	$7.95
00672534	Very Best of Oscar Peterson	$22.95
00672371	Bud Powell Classics	$19.95
00672376	Bud Powell Collection	$19.95
00672437	André Previn Collection	$19.95
00672507	Gonzalo Rubalcaba Collection	$19.95
00672303	Horace Silver Collection	$19.95
00672316	Art Tatum Collection	$22.95
00672355	Art Tatum Solo Book	$19.95
00672357	Billy Taylor Collection	$24.95
00673215	McCoy Tyner	$16.95
00672321	Cedar Walton Collection	$19.95
00672519	Kenny Werner Collection	$19.95
00672434	Teddy Wilson Collection	$19.95

SAXOPHONE
00673244	Julian "Cannonball" Adderley Collection	$19.95
00673237	Michael Brecker	$19.95
00672429	Michael Brecker Collection	$19.95
00672351	Brecker Brothers... And All Their Jazz	$19.95
00672447	Best of the Brecker Brothers	$19.95
00672315	Benny Carter Plays Standards	$22.95
00672314	Benny Carter Collection	$22.95
00672394	James Carter Collection	$19.95
00672349	John Coltrane Plays Giant Steps	$19.95
00672529	John Coltrane – Giant Steps	$14.95
00672494	John Coltrane – A Love Supreme	$14.95
00672493	John Coltrane Plays "Coltrane Changes"	$19.95
00672453	John Coltrane Plays Standards	$19.95
00673233	John Coltrane Solos	$22.95
00672328	Paul Desmond Collection	$19.95
00672454	Paul Desmond – Standard Time	$19.95
00672379	Eric Dolphy Collection	$19.95
00672530	Kenny Garrett Collection	$19.95
00699375	Stan Getz	$18.95
00672377	Stan Getz – Bossa Novas	$19.95
00672375	Stan Getz – Standards	$17.95
00673254	Great Tenor Sax Solos	$18.95
00672523	Coleman Hawkins Collection	$19.95
00673252	Joe Henderson – Selections from "Lush Life" & "So Near So Far"	$19.95
00672330	Best of Joe Henderson	$22.95

00673239	Best of Kenny G	$19.95
00673229	Kenny G – Breathless	$19.95
00672462	Kenny G – Classics in the Key of G	$19.95
00672485	Kenny G – Faith: A Holiday Album	$14.95
00672373	Kenny G – The Moment	$19.95
00672516	Kenny G – Paradise	$14.95
00672326	Joe Lovano Collection	$19.95
00672498	Jackie McLean Collection	$19.95
00672372	James Moody Collection – Sax and Flute	$19.95
00672416	Frank Morgan Collection	$19.95
00672539	Gerry Mulligan Collection	$19.95
00672352	Charlie Parker Collection	$19.95
00672444	Sonny Rollins Collection	$19.95
00675000	David Sanborn Collection	$16.95
00672528	Bud Shank Collection	$19.95
00672491	New Best of Wayne Shorter	$19.95
00672455	Lew Tabackin Collection	$19.95
00672334	Stanley Turrentine Collection	$19.95
00672524	Lester Young Collection	$19.95

TROMBONE
00672332	J.J. Johnson Collection	$19.95
00672489	Steve Turré Collection	$19.95

TRUMPET
00672480	Louis Armstrong Collection	$14.95
00672481	Louis Armstrong Plays Standards	$14.95
00672435	Chet Baker Collection	$19.95
00673234	Randy Brecker	$17.95
00672351	Brecker Brothers... And All Their Jazz	$19.95
00672447	Best of the Brecker Brothers	$19.95
00672448	Miles Davis – Originals, Vol. 1	$19.95
00672451	Miles Davis – Originals, Vol. 2	$19.95
00672450	Miles Davis – Standards, Vol. 1	$19.95
00672449	Miles Davis – Standards, Vol. 2	$19.95
00672479	Dizzy Gillespie Collection	$19.95
00673214	Freddie Hubbard	$14.95
00672382	Tom Harrell – Jazz Trumpet	$19.95
00672363	Jazz Trumpet Solos	$9.95
00672506	Chuck Mangione Collection	$19.95
00672525	Arturo Sandoval – Trumpet Evolution	$19.95

Prices and availability subject to change without notice.

0606

PLAY LIKE THE PROS

Jazz Guitar Instruction & Transcriptions from Hal Leonard

The Jazz Style of Tal Farlow
THE ELEMENTS OF BEBOP GUITAR
by Steve Rochinski

Finally, the book that defines the melodic and harmonic thinking behind the style of one of the most influential jazz guitarists of the 20th century, Tal Farlow. Includes instruction on: creating single-line solos; visualizing the neck; use of anticipation, expansion, and contraction; reharmonization; signature and chord voicings; chord-melody concepts; special signature effects such as bongos and harmonics; tune and solo transcriptions; and more!
00673245..$19.95

50 Essential Bebop Heads Arranged for Guitar

The best lines of Charlie Parker, Dizzy Gillespie, Thelonius Monk, and many more, for guitar with notes and tab. Includes: Donna Lee • Groovin' High • Ornithology • Confirmation • Epistrophy • and more.
00698990 ....$14.95

Jazz Guitar Chord Melodies
FOR SOLO GUITAR
arranged & performed by Dan Towey

This book/CD pack offers performance level chord-melody arrangements of 12 popular jazz songs for the solo guitarist. They range in difficulty from intermediate to advanced and include notes and tab. The CD includes complete solo performances. Songs include: All the Things You Are • Body and Soul • My Romance • How Insensitive • My One and Only Love • and more.
00698988 Book/CD Pack..$19.95

Chord Melody Standards for Guitar

15 great songs, including: Autumn in New York • Cheek to Cheek • Easy Living • Georgia on My Mind • The Girl from Ipanema • Have You Met Miss Jones? • Isn't It Romantic? • Stella by Starlight • The Way You Look Tonight • When I Fall in Love • When Sunny Gets Blue • more.
00699128..$9.95

Solo Jazz Guitar

The book starts with 11 lessons on chord melody concepts, then uses 20 familiar jazz standards to demonstrate these techniques, covering: diatonic and minor third substitution, contrary motion, back cycles, walking bass lines, modal chord scales, and more. Songs (in standard notation & TAB) include: All the Things You Are • Cherokee • Giant Steps • I Could Write a Book • Like Someone in Love • My Romance • Yesterdays • more.
00695317..$10.95

Best of Jazz Guitar
by Wolf Marshall
Signature Licks

Wolf Marshall provides a hands-on analysis of 10 of the most frequently played tunes in the jazz genre, as played by the leading guitarists of all time. Features: "St. Thomas" performed by Jim Hall, Tal Farlow and Kenny Burrell • "All Blues" performed by George Benson, Kenny Burrell and Pat Martino • "Satin Doll" performed by Howard Roberts and Joe Pass • "I'll Remember April" performed by Johnny Smith and Grant Green • and more!
00695586 Book/CD Pack..$24.95

101 Must-Know Jazz Licks
by Wolf Marshall
Signature Licks

Now you can add authentic jazz feel and flavor to your playing! Here are 101 definitive licks, plus a demonstration CD, from every major jazz guitar style, neatly organized into easy-to-use categories. They're all here: swing and pre-bop, bebop, post-bop modern jazz, hard bop and cool jazz, modal jazz, soul jazz and postmodern jazz. Includes an introduction by Wolf Marshall, tips for using the book and CD, and a listing of suggested recordings.
00695433 Book/CD Pack..$16.95

Jazz Guitar Improvisation
by Sid Jacobs

Develop your solo skills with this comprehensive method which includes a CD with 99 full demonstration tracks. Topics covered include: common jazz phrases; applying scales and arpeggios; guide tones, non-chordal tones, fourths; and more. Includes standard notation and tablature.
00695128 Book/CD Pack..$17.95

Joe Pass Collection

12 songs transcribed, including: Blues for Basie • Blues for Hank • Cheek to Cheek • Dissonance #1 • Happy Holiday Blues • I Got Rhythm • In a Sentimental Mood • Pasta Blues • Satin Doll • The Song Is You • The Way You Look Tonight • Yardbird Suite.
00672353..$18.95

JAZZ GUITAR GREATS

Learn the best lines of the masters! Each book/CD pack includes note-for-note legendary jazz performances transcribed and performed by Jack Grassel. The CD features two versions of each song at different tempos, with the rhythm section on a different channel. Includes standard notation and tablature.

Jazz Guitar Classics
Includes: Satin Doll/Kenny Burrell • Tangerine/Jimmy Raney • Honeysuckle Rose/Django Reinhardt • Billie's Bounce/George Benson • Stella by Starlight/Tal Farlow • Easy Living/Johnny Smith.
00698998 Book/CD Pack..$19.95

Jazz Guitar Favorites
Includes: All the Things That You Are/Hank Garland • I Hear a Symphony/Howard Roberts • Oleo/Pat Martino • Speak Low/Barney Kessel • When Sunny Gets Blue/George Barnes • Yesterdays/Wes Montgomery.
00698999 Book/CD Pack..$19.95

Jazz Guitar Standards
Includes: Falling in Love With You/Grant Green • I've Got You Under My Skin/Jim Hall • A Night in Tunisia/Billy Bauer • Stompin' at the Savoy/Charlie Christian • Yardbird Suite/Joe Pass • You Brought a New Kind of Love to Me/Chuck Wayne.
00672356 Book/CD Pack..$19.95

FOR MORE INFORMATION, SEE YOUR LOCAL MUSIC DEALER, OR WRITE TO:

HAL • LEONARD® CORPORATION
7777 W. BLUEMOUND RD. P.O. BOX 13819 MILWAUKEE, WI 53213
www.halleonard.com

Prices, contents and availability subject to change without notice.